In association with abkco Music, Inc.
© 2004 abkco Music Inc.
Book published by abkco Music, Inc.

SAM COOKE

4	ANOTHER SATURDAY NIGHT
14	BASIN STREET BLUES
18	BRING IT ON HOME TO ME
9	CHAIN GANG
20	A CHANGE IS GONNA COME
24	COUSIN OF MINE
28	CUPID
38	(SOMEBODY) EASE MY TROUBLIN' MIND
31	EVERYBODY LOVES TO CHA CHA CHA
48	FALLING IN LOVE
42	(I LOVE YOU) FOR SENTIMENTAL REASONS
53	(AIN'T THAT) GOOD NEWS
58	GOOD TIMES
66	HAVING A PARTY
70	HOME (WHEN SHADOWS FALL)
198	I'LL COME RUNNING BACK TO YOU
63	I'M JUST A COUNTRY BOY
78	IT'S GOT THE WHOLE WORLD SHAKIN'
86	JESUS GAVE ME WATER
90	JUST FOR YOU
83	KEEP MOVIN' ON
96	LITTLE RED ROOSTER
102	LOVABLE
110	MEET ME AT MARY'S PLACE
107	NOTHING CAN CHANGE THIS LOVE
114	ONLY SIXTEEN
118	THE RIDDLE SONG
122	ROME (WASN'T BUILT IN A DAY)
126	SAD MOOD
140	SHAKE
132	SITTIN' IN THE SUN
136	SUGAR DUMPLING
145	SUMMERTIME
148	TENNESSEE WALTZ
154	THAT'S WHERE IT'S AT
157	THERE'LL BE NO SECOND TIME
162	TOUCH THE HEM OF HIS GARMENT
172	TRY A LITTLE LOVE
178	TWISTIN' THE NIGHT AWAY
182	WHEN A BOY FALLS IN LOVE
165	WIN YOUR LOVE FOR ME
186	(WHAT A) WONDERFUL WORLD
190	YEAH MAN
193	YOU SEND ME
74	YOU WERE MADE FOR ME
203	YOU'RE NOBODY 'TIL SOMEBODY LOVES YOU

Folio Editors Alisa Coleman-Ritz & Carol Cuellar/Art Director Iris Keitel/Cover Illustration Angelo Tillery (based on a photo by Jess Rand ©Michaelochs.com)/Cover Design Bonfilio Design/Art Production Janessa Gursky
Music Transcription Coordinators Dale Park & Richard DeCicco/Concept Lenne Allik

ANOTHER SATURDAY NIGHT

Words and Music by
SAM COOKE

Moderately ♩ = 120

Chorus:

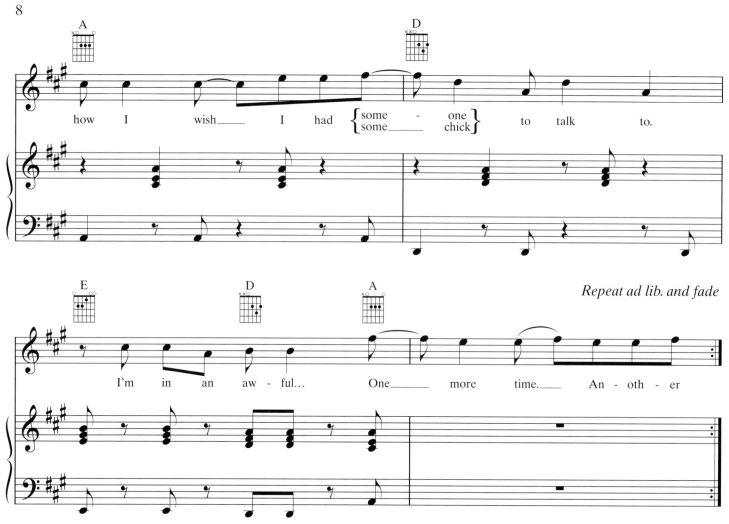

Verse 2:
Now, another fella told me,
He had a sister who looked just fine.
Instead of being my deliverance,
(Spoken:) She had a strange resemblance
To a cat named Frankenstein.
Here…
(To Chorus:)

Verse 3:
It's a hard on a fella,
When he don't know his way around.
If I don't find me a honey
To help me spend my money,
I'm gonna have to blow this town,
Here it's…
(To Chorus:)

CHAIN GANG

Words and Music by
SAM COOKE

Chain Gang - 5 - 1
PFM0316

10 *Chorus:*

BASIN STREET BLUES

Words and Music by
SPENCER WILLIAMS

BRING IT ON HOME TO ME

Words and Music by
SAM COOKE

ev - er_____ change_ your mind_____ a - bout leav - in', leav - in' me be -
2.3.4.5.6. *See additional lyrics*

Bring It on Home to Me - 2 - 1
PFM0316

Verse 2:
I know I laughed when you left,
But now I know I only hurt myself.
Baby, bring it to me, bring your sweet lovin',
Bring it on home to me,
Yeah, (yeah,) yeah, (yeah,) yeah, (yeah.)

Verse 3:
I'll give you jewelry and money, too,
That ain't all, that ain't all I'll do for you,
Baby, if you bring it to me, bring your sweet lovin',
Bring it on home to me,
Yeah, (yeah,) yeah, (yeah,) yeah, (yeah.)

Verse 4:
You know I'll always be your slave
'Til I'm buried, buried in my grave.
Oh, honey, bring it to me, bring your sweet lovin',
Bring it on home to me,
Yeah, (yeah,) yeah, (yeah,) yeah, (yeah.)

Verse 5:
(One more thing:) I tried to treat you right,
But you stayed out, stayed out in night, but I'll forgive you.
Bring it to me, bring your sweet lovin',
Bring it on home to me,
Yeah, (yeah,) yeah, (yeah,) yeah, (yeah.)
Yeah, (yeah,) yeah, (yeah,) yeah, *(etc.)*
(Vocal ad lib. and fade)

A CHANGE IS GONNA COME

Words and Music by
SAM COOKE

Verse 2:
It's been too hard living but I'm afraid to die
'Cause I don't know what's up there beyond the sky.
It's been a long, a long time comin',
But I know, oh-oo-oh,
A change gonna come, oh yes, it will.

Verse 4:
There've been times that I thought
I couldn't last for long
But now I think I'm able to carry on
It's been a long, a long time comin',
but I know, oh-oo-oh, a change gonna come, oh yes, it will.

COUSIN OF MINE

Words and Music by
SAM COOKE

Chorus:

CUPID

Words and Music by
SAM COOKE

EVERYBODY LOVES TO CHA CHA CHA

Words and Music by
SAM COOKE

Verse 1:

1. Took my ba - by to the hop last night;___ and what to my sur - prise,___

when we got there, she hit me with the news,___

right be - tween the eyes,___ yeah.___ She said she could - n't do___ the

cha, cha, cha.___ She said she could - n't do___ the cha, cha, cha.___ She could - n't...

36

Verse 4:

(Somebody)
EASE MY TROUBLIN' MIND

Words and Music by
SAM COOKE

Verse 3.
I wish my baby would come and tell me ev'rything's alright, yeah.
I sure wish my baby would come and tell me ev'rything is still alright, oh yes, I do.
(To Bridge:)

Verse 4:
Why won't somebody come and ease my troublin' mind?
Yeah.
I sure wish somebody would come and ease my troublin' mind,
Oh yeah.

(I Love You)
FOR SENTIMENTAL REASONS

Words by
DEEK WATSON

Music by
WILLIAM BEST

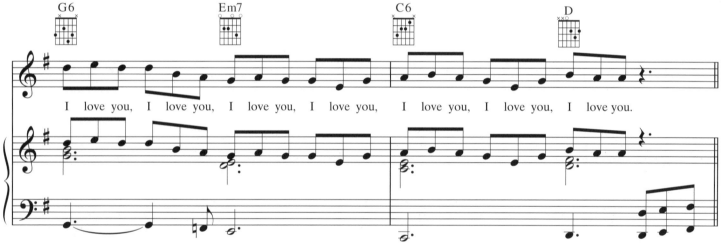

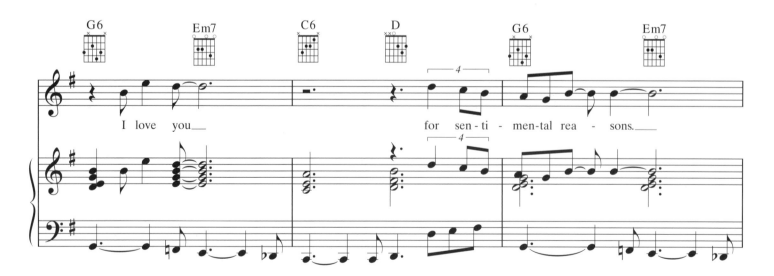

(I Love You) For Sentimental Reasons - 6 - 1
PFM0316

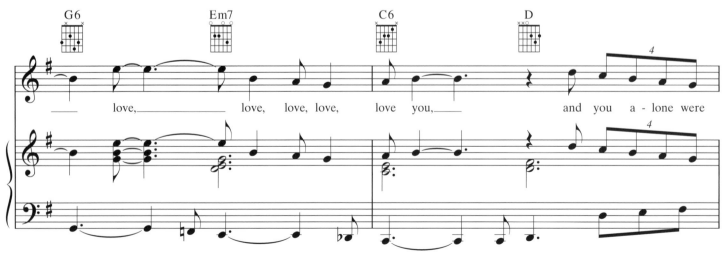

think of you ___ ev - 'ry morn - ing; _____ I dream of you ev - er - y, ev - er - y,

ev - er - y, ev - er - y night; ___ and I know ___ I'm nev - er lone - ly ___ When-

tacet

ev - er you are ___ in sight. ___ I know, I know, I know I ___

___ love, ___ love, love, love, love you, ___ and you a - lone were

46

FALLING IN LOVE

Words and Music by
HAROLD BATTISTE

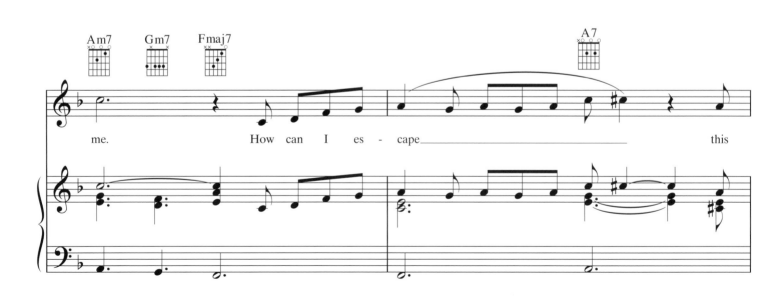

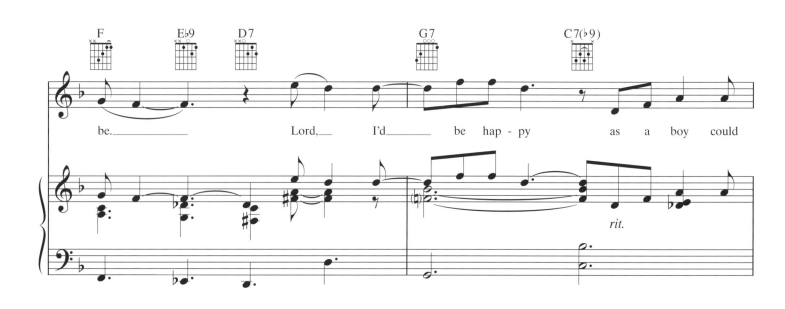

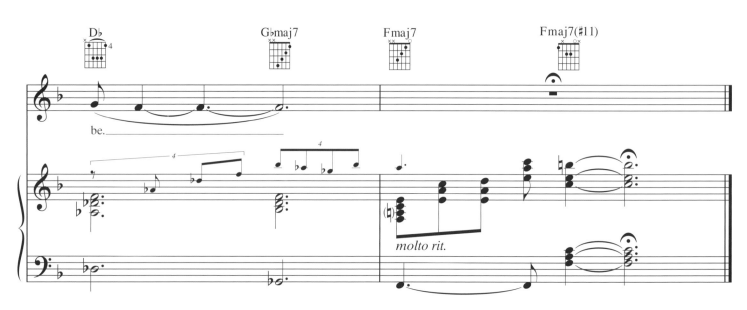

(Ain't That)
GOOD NEWS

Words and Music by
SAM COOKE

GOOD TIMES

Words and Music by
SAM COOKE

Moderate shuffle ♩ = 120

Woh, _____ la, la, ta, da. _____ No, _____
La, la, _____ la, la, ta, da. _____ La, da, la, ta,

la, ta, da. _____ La, la, la, all night long, _____ yeah. _____

2.

yeah.

Chorus:

Come on _____ and let the good time roll. _____

62

I'M JUST A COUNTRY BOY

Words and Music by
MARSHALL BARER and
FRED HELLERMAN

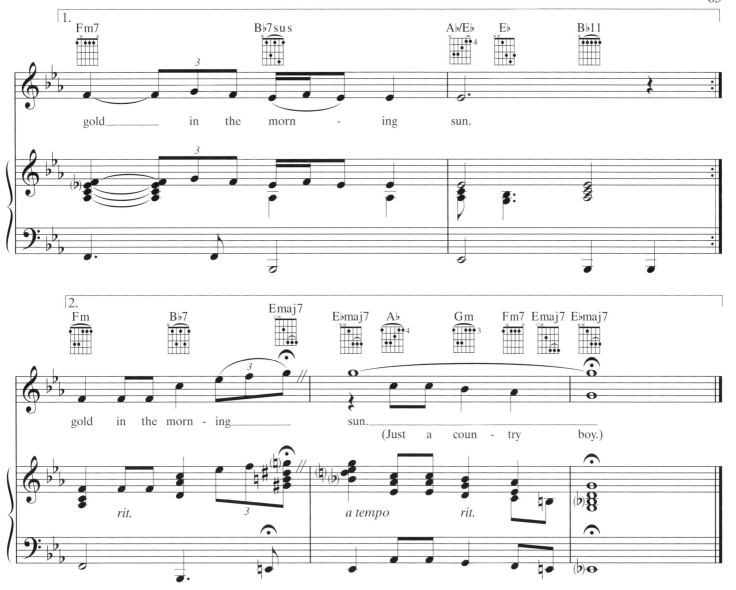

Verse 2:
I'm never gonna kiss the ruby lips
Of the prettiest girl in town.
No, I'm never gonna ask her if she'd marry me
For I know she'd turn me down.

Chorus 2:
'Cause I'm just a country boy.
Money, money have I none.
Oh, but I've got that silver in the stars
And gold in the morning sun.
I have gold in the morning sun.
(Just a country boy.)

HAVING A PARTY

Words and Music by
SAM COOKE

Medium rock swing ♩ = 132

Verse:

1. We're hav-ing a par-ty,____ danc-ing to the
2. *See additional lyrics*

mu - sic____ played____ by the D. J.____

Verse 2:
Everybody's swinging,
Sally's doin' that twist, now.
If you take requests,
I've got a few for you.
Play that song called "Soul Twist,"
Play that one called "I Know,"
Don't forget them "Mashed Potatoes,"
No other songs will do.
(To Chorus:)

HOME
(When Shadows Fall)

Words and Music by
GEOFF CLARKSON, HARRY CLARKSON
and PETER VAN STEEDEN

YOU WERE MADE FOR ME

Words and Music by
SAM COOKE

IT'S GOT THE WHOLE WORLD SHAKIN'

Words and Music by
SAM COOKE

Moderate rock ♩ = 144

It's got the

It's Got the Whole World Shakin' - 5 - 1
PFM0316

2.

G   A

Well, it makes you wig - gle, makes you move,__

__ puts your bod - y

in the groove.__ You move to hol -

ler, oh, you wan - na shout.__

It's Got the Whole World Shakin' - 5 - 4
PFM0316

KEEP MOVIN' ON

Words and Music by
SAM COOKE

Verse 2:
Brother, mind what you do
And how your treat your fellow man.
If you knew like me you'd try to live
The very best you can.
For if you spread good all around
You'd be able to sleep when the sun go down.
(To Chorus:)

JESUS GAVE ME WATER

Words and Music by
LUCIE E. CAMPBELL

Moderately ♩ = 92

Chorus:

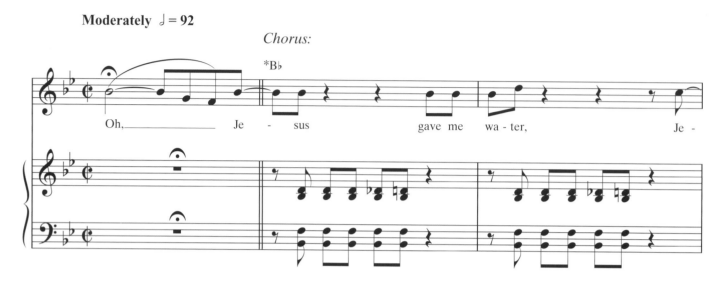

Oh,_____ Je - sus gave me wa - ter, Je-

sus gave me wa - ter, Je - sus gave me

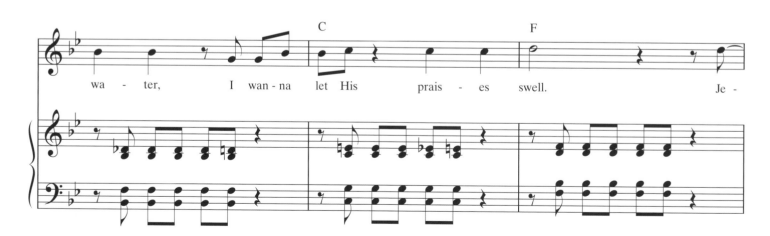

wa - ter, I wan - na let His prais - es swell. Je-

*The chord symbols represent the harmonies outlined in the a capella gospel choir.

Jesus Gave Me Water - 4 - 1
PFM0316

88

Jesus Gave Me Water - 4 - 3
PFM0316

Verse 2:
Well, on that woman He had pity,
She ran back to the city,
Crying, "Glory, Hallelujah!"
And did His wonders tell.
She left my Savior singing,
She came back to Him bringing
The time she had her water, Lord,
And it was not in the well.
(To Chorus:)

Verse 3:
Lord, that woman left for shoutin',
There was no room for doubtin'
That she had met her Savior,
Who did her wonders tell.
Every time she'd doubt Him,
She'd start to think about Him,
The man that gave her that water, Lord,
And it was not in the well.
(To Chorus:)

JUST FOR YOU

Words and Music by
SAM COOKE

LITTLE RED ROOSTER

Written by
WILLIE DIXON

Moderate blues ♩. = 92

Verse 1:

1. I got a lit-tle red roost-er too la-zy to crow for days.____

Verse 3:

Verse 4:

LOVABLE

Words and Music by
SAM COOKE and
TONY HARRIS

NOTHING CAN CHANGE THIS LOVE

Words and Music by
SAM COOKE

noth-in',___ noth-in' can___ ev-er change this love I have___ for

you.___ 2. Ooh,_____ make me

Oh,_____ you're the

Bridge:

ap-ple___ of my eye._____ You're cher-ry pie.___

MEET ME AT MARY'S PLACE

Words and Music by
SAM COOKE

Easy swing ♩ = 104

1. A

Verse:

friend of mine told__ me one ear - ly morn,__ (O - ver at Mar - y's place,__
2. *See additional lyrics*

___ oh.) said, "To - night there's gon - na be a par - ty go - in' on."__

Meet Me at Mary's Place - 4 - 1
PFM0316

112

ONLY SIXTEEN

Words and Music by
SAM COOKE

THE RIDDLE SONG

Words and Music by
SAM COOKE

ROME
(Wasn't Built in a Day)

Words and Music by
SAM COOKE and
BETTY & BEVERLY PRUDHOMME

Moderately ♩ = 126

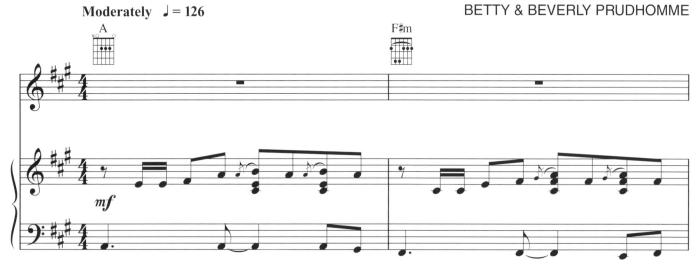

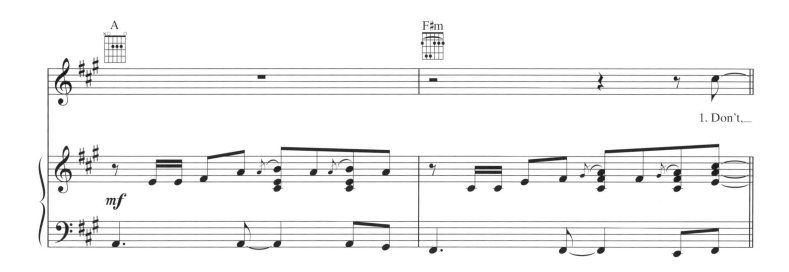

Rome (Wasn't Built in a Day) - 4 - 1
PFM0316

Rome (Wasn't Built in a Day) - 4 - 2
PFM0316

SAD MOOD

Words and Music by
SAM COOKE

Moderately ♩ = 100

Chorus 1:

I'm___ in a sad___ mood to-night;

oh,___ I'm in a sad___ mood.___ I'm in a sad___

128

SITTIN' IN THE SUN

Words and Music by
IRVING BERLIN

134

SUGAR DUMPLING

Words and Music by
SAM COOKE

Chorus:

Sug-ar Dump-ling,__ you my ba-by. I love you in ev-'ry way.__

Sug-ar Dump-ling,__ you my ba-by. My love grows strong-er ev-'ry day. Yeah.__

Verse 2:
Whenever I tell her, honey, I'm hungry,
Now go and fix me something to eat,
This girl rushes in the kitchen and fixes me a dinner
With seven different kinds of meat.
If I call her up at two o'clock in the morning
And say come on over if you can,
Before I hang up the telephone, she's sitting beside me
With a cup of coffee in her hand.
(To Chorus:)

SHAKE

Words and Music by
SAM COOKE

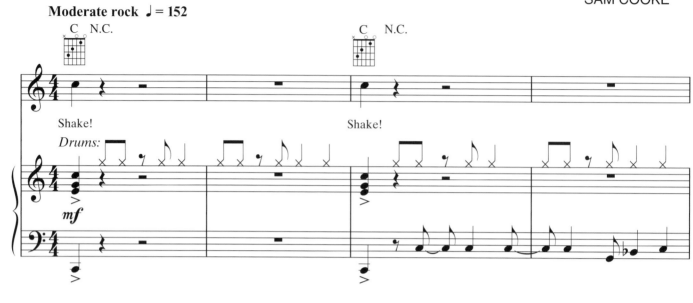

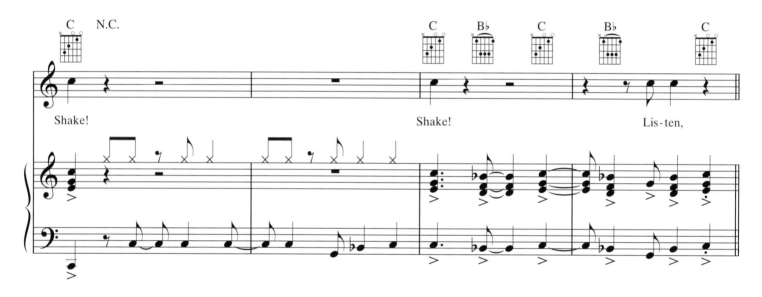

142

SUMMERTIME

Words and Music by
GEORGE GERSHWIN,
DuBOSE and DOROTHY HEYWARD
and IRA GERSHWIN

Summertime - 3 - 1
PFM0316

D.S. % and fade on ad lib.

2. One of these

Verse 2:
One of these mornings, you're gonna rise up singing.
Then you'll spread your wings and take to the sky.
But until that morning, there is nothing can harm you,
With Daddy and Mommy standing by.
(To ad lib. humming:)

TENNESSEE WALTZ

Words and Music by
REDD STEWART
and PEE WEE KING

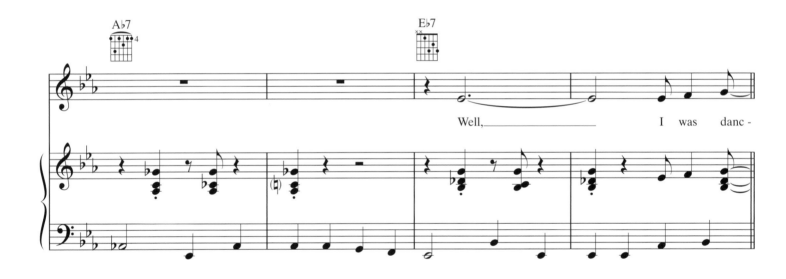

Well,_____ I was danc-

in'   with my ba - by_____   to that Ten-

150

they were danc - in',___ my friend___
stole my sweet - heart___ a - way___
from me. Oh, yes, he did.___ Well, I re - mem -
ber___ the___ night___ and that beau -

Tennessee Waltz - 6 - 3
PFM0316

THAT'S WHERE IT'S AT

Words and Music by
SAM COOKE and
J.W. ALEXANDER

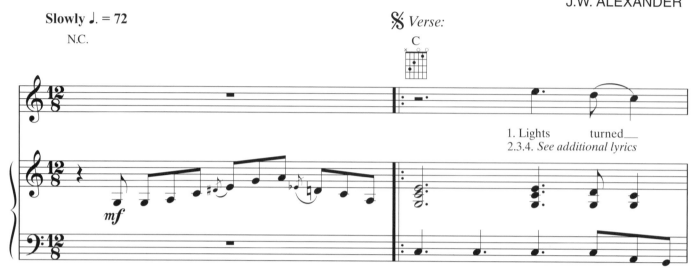

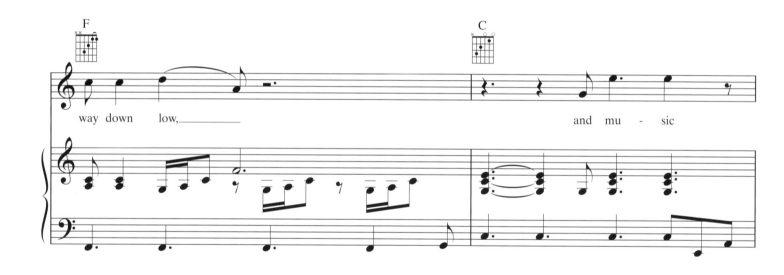

That's Where It's At - 3 - 1
PFM0316

That's where___ it's at,_____ oh, yeah, (oh, yeah,) and oh,

yeah, (and oh, yeah.) Let me tell you this one thing. _____

Verse 2:
Your world turned upside down,
You're makin' not a sound,
No one else around;
That's where it's at, yeah, let me tell ya.

Verse 3:
Your heart beatin' fast,
You're knowin' that time will pass,
But a-hopin' that it lasts;
That's where it's at, oh, yeah.
(To Chorus:)

Verse 4:
To say, "It's time to go,"
And she says, "Yes, I know,
But just stay one minute more."
That's where it's at, oh, let me say it one more time.
(To Chorus:)

THERE'LL BE NO SECOND TIME

Words and Music by
CLIFTON WHITE

Verse 2:
I was a fool to give my love
'Cause you swore you'd love me by the stars above.
But you walked out and left me behind.
So there'll be no, no second time.
(To Bridge:)

TOUCH THE HEM OF HIS GARMENT

Words and Music by
SAM COOKE

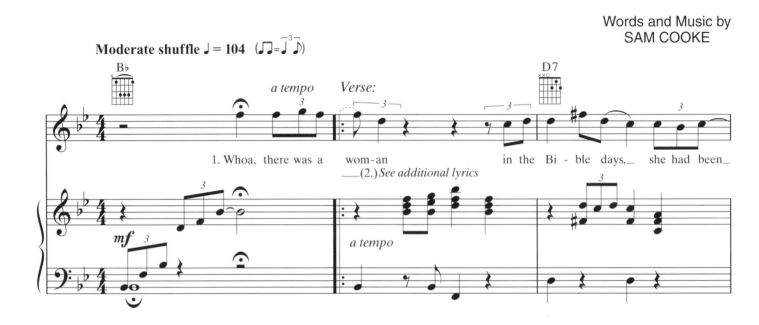

Verse 2:
Whoa, she spent her money here and there
Until she had no, had no more to spare.
The doctors they done all that they could
But their medicine would do no good.
When she touched Him, the Savior didn't see.
But still he turned around and cried,
"Somebody touched me."
She said, "It was I who just wanna touch the hem of your garment.
I know I'll be made whole right now."

Chorus 2:
She stood there crying, "Oh, Lord! Oh, Lord! Oh-oo-oh,
Oh, Lord! Oh, Lord!"
She said, "If I could just touch the hem of your garment,
I know I'll be made whole right now."

WIN YOUR LOVE FOR ME

Words and Music by
SAM COOKE

Verse 1:

1. Man-y's the day___ I've___ longed for you,___ to hold you in___ my___ arms; man-y's the night___ I've___ cried for you,___ and for your man-y charms. If you'd on-ly come___ to me,___ my heart___ would-n't be full of sor-row; but

Chorus:

now, all I can do is hope and pray that you'll come to me to-

mor - row. Whoa, whoa, lit - tle girl,

how hap - py I would be if some

mir - a - cle could win your love for me. Win your

Verse 2:

TRY A LITTLE LOVE

Words and Music by
SAM COOKE and
J.W. ALEXANDER

174

Verse 3:

Verse 4:

TWISTIN' THE NIGHT AWAY

Words and Music by
SAM COOKE

Moderate rock swing ♩ = 144

Verse:

1. Let_____ me tell you 'bout a place_____
2. Here's_____ a man in eve - ning clothes._____
3. *See additional lyrics*

some - where up in New York way_____
How_____ he got here I don't know, but

Chorus:

Verse 3:
Here's a fellow in blue jeans
Dancing with an older queen
Whose dolled up in-a diamond rings
And twisting the night away.
Man, you oughta see her go,
Twistin' to the rock and roll.
Here you'll find the young and old
Twistin' the night away.
(To Chorus:)

WHEN A BOY FALLS IN LOVE

Words and Music by
SAM COOKE and
CLINTON LAVERT

I've heard them say love___ was a won-der-ful thing,___ some-thing

you could-n't hide___ on a shelf. But to me, they no long-er have to ex-plain, be-

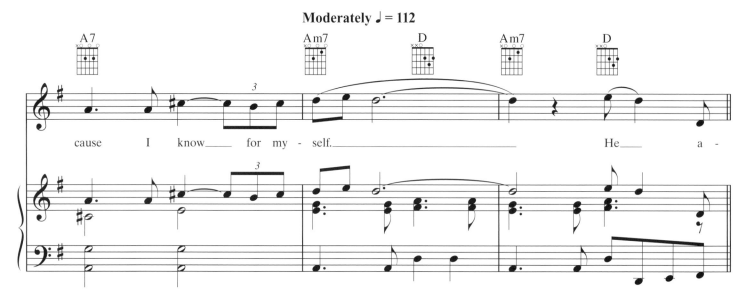

cause I know___ for my-self.___ He___ a-

184

(What a)
WONDERFUL WORLD

Words and Music by
SAM COOKE, HERB ALPERT
and LOU ADLER

(What a) Wonderful World - 4 - 4
PFM0316

YEAH MAN

Words and Music by
SAM COOKE

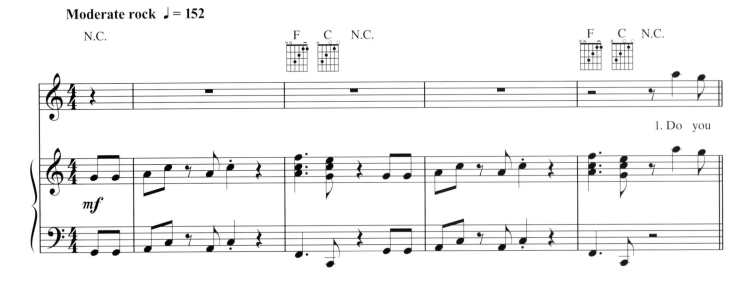

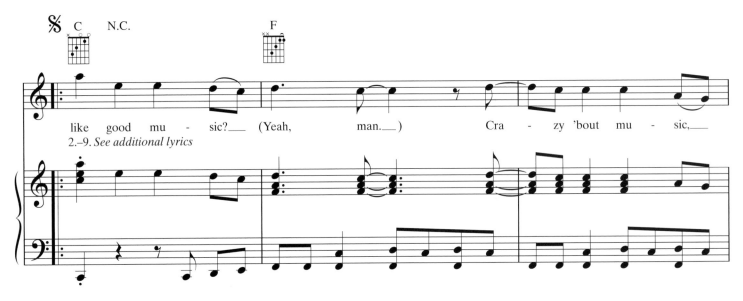

Yeah Man - 3 - 1
PFM0316

Coda

Swim - min', swim - min'.
(Yeah, man.___) (Yeah, man.___)

got to go, I'm goin' home.
(Yeah, man.___) (Yeah, man.___) (Yeah, man.___)

Verse 2:
Do you like all the dances? (Yeah, man.)
Crazy 'bout the dances. (Yeah, man.)
Long as it's swingin'. (Yeah, man.)
What? (Yeah, man.) What? (Yeah, man.)

Verse 3:
Let's try some of the dances. (Yeah, man.)
I don't know which one, now. (Yeah, man.)
Let's try to do the Monkey. (Yeah, man.)
Alright? (Yeah, man.) Yeah. (Yeah, man.)

Verse 4:
Do you like all the dances? (Yeah, man.)
Crazy 'bout the dances. (Yeah, man.)
Let's try a new dance. (Yeah, man.)
(Yeah, man.) (Yeah, man.)

Verse 5:
Let's try the Watusi. (Yeah, man.)
I love to do the 'Tusi. (Yeah, man.)
Put the Twist with the 'Tusi. (Yeah, man.)
(Yeah, man.) (Yeah, man.)

Verse 6:
Now, let's try a new dance. (Yeah, man.)
Dig what I tell ya. (Yeah, man.)
Got to do what I tell ya. (Yeah, man.)
Gonna do it? (Yeah, man.) (Yeah, man.)

Verse 7:
You're on a football field, now. (Yeah, man.)
Down in the huddle. (Yeah, man.)
Run for that touchdown. (Yeah, man.)
(Yeah, man.) (Yeah, man.)

Verse 8:
You on a baseball field, now. (Yeah, man.)
The bat's in your hand, girl. (Yeah, man.)
Swing for that homerun. (Yeah, man.)
(Yeah, man.) (Yeah, man.)

Verse 9:
You in the middle of an ocean. (Yeah, man.)
The ship is goin' down, now. (Yeah, man.)
Swim for your life, now. (Yeah, man.)
Yeah, (Yeah, man.) yeah. (Yeah, man.)
(*To Coda*)

You Send Me

Words and Music by
SAM COOKE

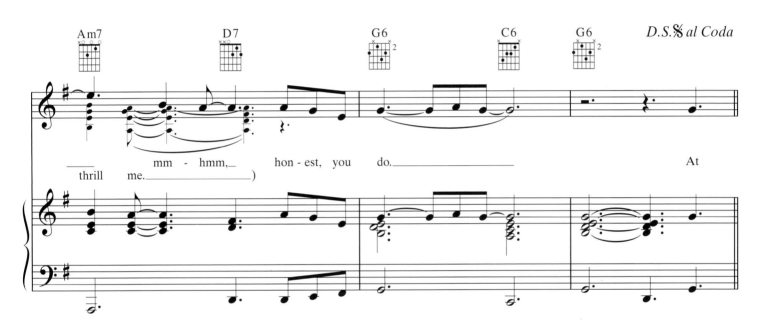

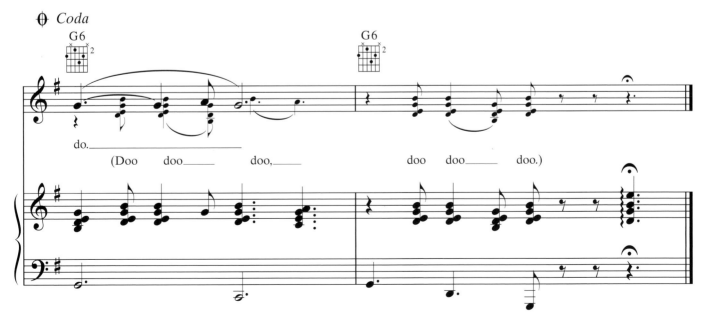

I'LL COME RUNNING BACK TO YOU

Words and Music by
WILLIAM COOK

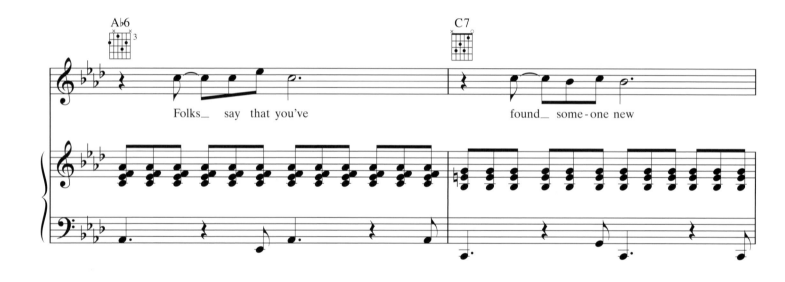

Folks__ say that you've found__ some-one new

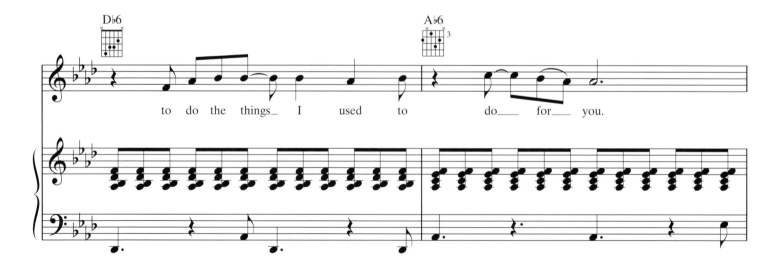

to do the things__ I used to do__ for__ you.

Just call my name, whoa,_____ I know I'm__ not a - shamed;_

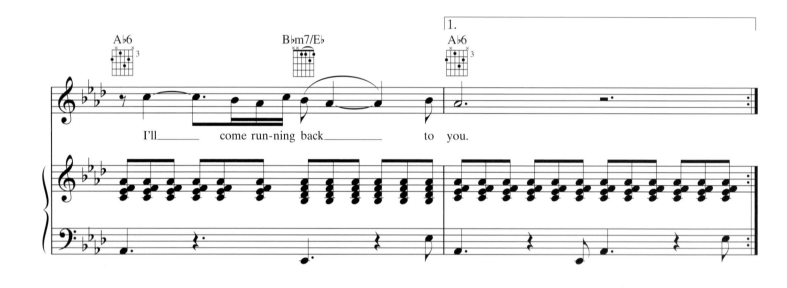

I'll_____ come run-ning back_____ to you.

you.

YOU'RE NOBODY 'TIL SOMEBODY LOVES YOU

Words and Music by
RUSS MORGAN, LARRY STOCK
and JAMES CAVANAUGH

You're Nobody 'Til Somebody Loves You - 5 - 1
PFM0316

Some Artists Made Mu
Sam Cooke Made Hist

JESUS GAVE ME WATER • TO CH THE HEM OF HIS G
I'LL COME RUNNING BAC   • LOVABLE • Y
ME • (I LOVE YOU) FOR   NTAL REASONS
SIXTEEN • YOU WERE MAD   • WIN YOUR LOV
EVERYBODY LOVES TO C   CHA • WONDERFU
SUMMERTIME • CHAIN   D MOOD • CUPID •
THE NIGHT AW   BRING IT ON
ME • NOTH   OVE • LIT
ROOSTER •   • SUGAR D
AIN'T THAT   ALTZ • MEE

Nearly 40 years after his last record, Sam C
continues to influence generation after ger

From gospel to new wave, from rockers to rappers, nearly every form of popu
bears the unmistakable imprint of the legendary Sam Cooke. The infectious
smooth styling, and of course, that incredible voice. Now the legend that is S
again on DVD and hybrid Super Audio Compact Discs™ using DSD™ technolo

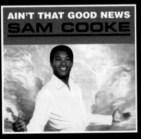

Ain't That Good News
- The first of his Tracey Records imprint
- Restored and remastered Hybrid SACD
- Available for the first time on Compact Disc
- 12 tracks

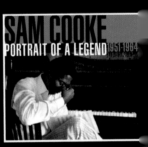

Keep Movin' On
- Restored and remastered Hybrid SACD
- Repackaged
- 22 tracks including "A CHANGE IS GONNA COME"

LEGEND DVD
Extended version of the critically acclaimed VH-1 Sam Cooke Legends Over two hours of additional interviews with Aretha Franklin, Bobby Womack, Lou Rawls, Lloyd Price, Lou Adler, L.C. Cooke and more! Featuring rare and never-before-seen performance clips, TV footage and family photos.

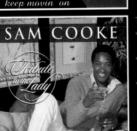

Tribute To The Lady
- Restored and remastered Hybrid SACD
- Available for the first time on Compact Disc
- 21 tracks

Not available in the United States & Canada